D1191366

CLAIRE AND EMMA

Claire and Emma

Diana Peter

Photographs by Jeremy Finlay

The John Day Company   New York

Copyright © 1976 by A & C Black Ltd. All rights reserved.
First United States edition 1977
Designed by Ruth Prentice. Printed in Great Britain.
0–381–90059–2 (RB)   CIP in the back of the book

This is Claire. She is four.

This is her sister Emma, who is two.

Here they are with their mother and their big brother, Alastair, who is six.

Both Claire and Emma were born deaf, which means that they can't hear.

They are learning to speak, which takes a long time if you can't hear.

Claire and Emma have a friend called Charlotte who often comes to play with them.

Claire and Emma each wear a hearing aid,
which helps them become aware of sounds.

It is made up of four pieces:

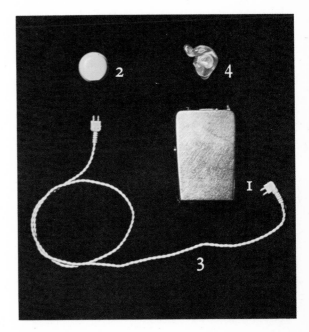

1 This picks up sounds and
multiplies them; it is called the
amplifier.

2 This passes the sounds into the ear;
it is called the receiver.

3 This wire goes between the
amplifier and the receiver.

4 This is an "ear mould" that fits into
the ear. If it falls out of the ear,
it makes a strange whistling sound.

Claire wears one hearing aid, and Emma
wears two. This is because Claire is slightly more
aware of loud sounds.

Their hearing aids sometimes get in the way, or
even fall out if they are romping around.

Claire watches your mouth very
carefully, and is learning to
understand what it means when
your lips move in a certain way.
This is called lip-reading.

It is very difficult to lip-read well.
You can help Claire by speaking
clearly.

"Push."

Claire likes climbing trees, but her sense of balance is not very good. (Our sense of balance depends on our ears.)

Charlotte finds it hard to call Claire down.
Until Claire looks at Charlotte's face, she won't know what Charlotte wants her to do.

Alastair wants to say he's sorry to
Claire, but he's finding it difficult.

He will have to wait until she stops
crying and looks at him.

Of course, a deaf person can't hear a knock at the door,
or listen to the radio, or use the telephone.

Claire enjoys television, but she cannot understand it all.
Someone has to explain the story to her more clearly.

It is hard to lip-read from people on television.
They talk too quickly and often look away, so that you
can't see their lips.

Some of the sounds you make don't show on your lips. And many sounds look alike on your lips when you say them.

For example, *pen*, *Ben*, and *men* all look alike. *Share* and *chair* look alike. *Ham* looks like *am*. *Hill* looks like *ill*, *hand* looks like *and*—and there are lots of others too.

Claire likes doing the same things
that the rest of the family enjoy.

Claire and Emma are both learning to swim. They have a lot of fun in the water.

Claire has many friends, and she
likes to join in all their games.

Claire cannot always make herself understood, as her speech is not very clear. If you don't quite understand her, try to help her explain. Don't be in a hurry and don't walk away if you cannot understand at first. Just give her a little longer.

Claire and Emma have a lot of extra lessons to help them speak well. They have a special machine called a "speech trainer."

If Claire blows, it helps her to use her lungs properly for speaking. Claire enjoys these lessons, as her speech trainer makes the sounds louder than her hearing aid does. But listening is hard work if you're not used to it.

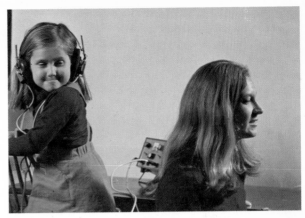

On school mornings, Claire and Alastair get themselves
dressed, while their mother helps Emma. The family has
breakfast together. Emma often spills her milk, or
Claire knocks over the packet of cereal.

Her mother gets angry, but Claire doesn't really
understand that she is cross, and just laughs.

Claire goes to a school where there are only six other deaf children in her class. So she gets the extra teaching she needs.

A lot of the time they mix with the other children in the school who can hear.

Claire is taken to and from school by taxi, as she has farther to go than most children.

Emma doesn't go to school yet.
A teacher comes once a week to
help her learn to lip-read. On the
other days her mother gives her
a lesson.

After their bath, Emma and Claire and Alastair have a bedtime story

Claire and Emma like doing just the
same things as other children,
and they like people to be friendly
and talk with them, so that they
don't feel left out.

Library of Congress Cataloging in Publication Data

Peter, Diana.
   Claire and Emma.

   SUMMARY: Text and photographs introduce two deaf
sisters who are learning to lip-read and speak.
   1. Children, Deaf—Juv. lit. 2. Deaf—
Means of communication—Juv. lit. 3. Brothers
and sisters—Juv. lit. [1. Deaf. 2. Physi-
cally handicapped. 3. Brothers and sisters] I. Finlay,
Jeremy. II. Title
HV2380. P46   1977   362.7'8'42   77-629
ISBN 0-381-90059-2 RB

DATE DUE

FEB 1 0 1983		
DEC 0 6 1985		
NOV 1 1 1987		
FEB 2 3 1995		
MAY 0 1 1996		
OCT 2 8 1987		
MAR 1 1 2012		